THE TRANSFER TREE

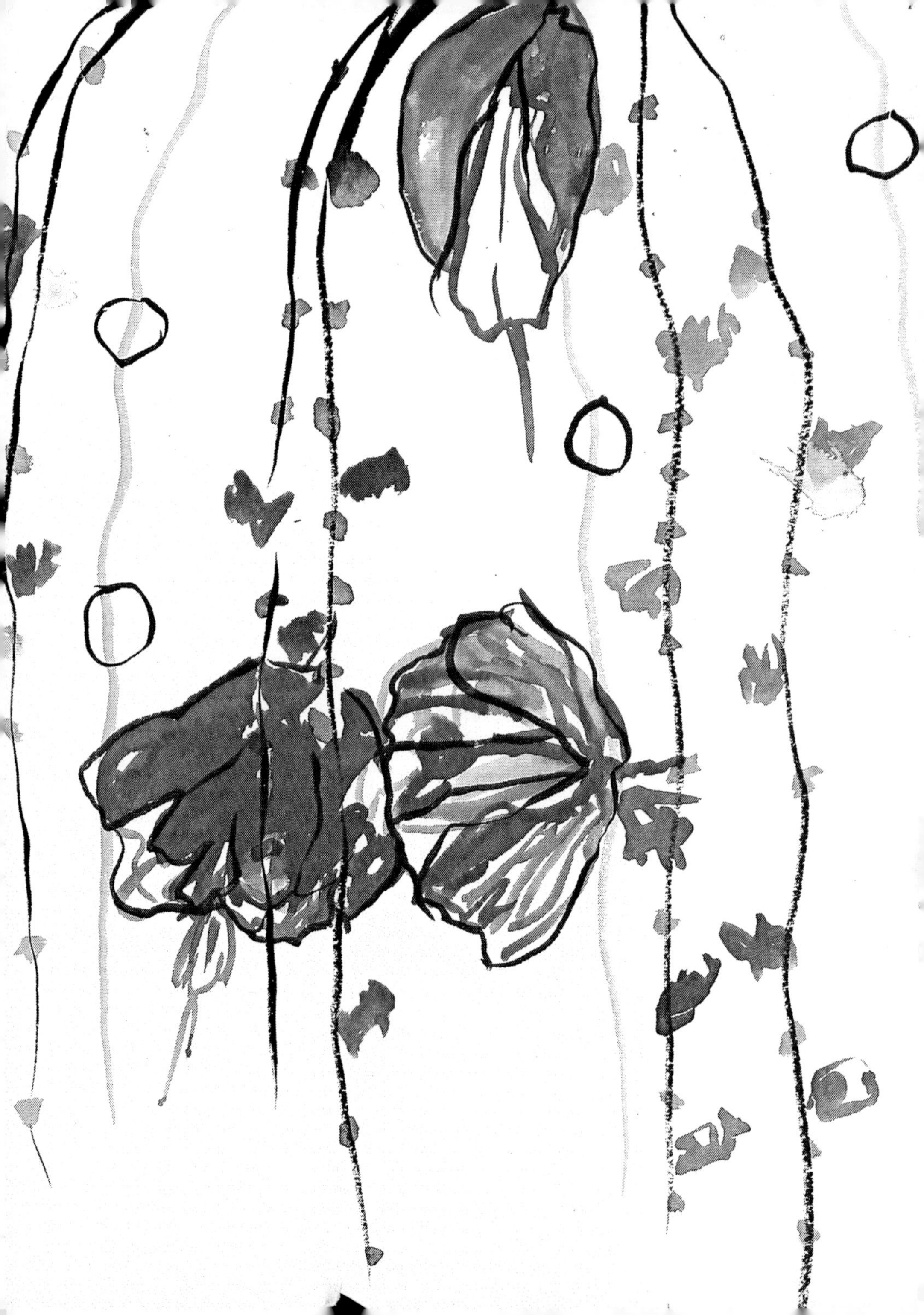

THE TRANSFER TREE

KAREN YOUTZ

1913 Press
www.1913press.org
1913press@gmail.com

1913 is a not-for-profit collective.
Contributions to 1913 Press may be tax-deductible.

Manufactured in the oldest country in the world, The United States of America.

Many thanks to all the artists, from this century and the last,
who made this project possible.

This publication is supported in generous part by individual donors,
named & unnamed:
Anonymous (x9), Robert J. Bertholf, Richard Dillard, Ectopistes Migratorius,
Kathleen Ossip, Coco Owen, Christopher Nealon, Marjorie Perloff,
Jean-Jacques Poucel, Matvei Yankelevich.

1913 thanks Le Board:
Eleanor Antin, Rae Armantrout, Thalia Field, Scarlett Higgins, Jen Hofer,
Matthew Hofer, Fanny Howe, Joseph Jeon, John Keene, Sawako Nakayasu,
Claudia Rankine, Jerome Rothenberg, Cole Swensen, John Yau.

Founder & Editrice: Sandra Doller
Vice-editor & Designer: Ben Doller

ISBN: 9780984029730
Cover art by Monisha Lundquist

19
3
13

CONTENTS

THE FIELD'S UNSECRET NET	5
PUBLIC FRUIT	6
PURPLE TREE	7
NORMAL ANGELS	10
EACH SENSE IS A STAR	11
THE CROSS WAS BAD MOJO	12
WHY I AM RELUCTANT TO SET A WEDDING DATE	14
THE GREEN INSIDE THE SUN	17
STARLET	19
CANNOT BE TRANSPORTED OR PRESERVED	20
FELT SENSE RECONVENES	21
FIELD HERE	22
AN "EARTH OF LIGHT" THE LIFE FORCE UNFORCED	24
NO NEED	26
SYMBOLS ARE INTERNAL FACTS	27
SONG CONTEST	28
WHITE TREE IN NAVY SPACE	29
COVERED WITH ASHES?	30
RESTLESS	32
THROUGH	34
THIS IS THE VERSO	35
PAIN HAS MINIONS-ARMIES	36
ASHES FALL FROM THE SKY	38
PEEK OUT OF THE BLACK HOOD INTO ABJECT DARKNESS, FEEL FURTHER (THE SPLIT BRANCH'S FIST-SIZED BOLE)	39

NO SUBSTANCE NO DARKNESS	41
THE BLACK FIRE	43
NATIVITY	44
URSA MAJOR AND URSA MINOR	46
THE BINDING OF THE BUD	47
HOW NOT TO BE BORN	48
RAPIDITY	49
BY ACCIDENT TRACKING HIM WHERE HE WENT	51
RARE MINERAL AND THE SOCIAL STRUCTURE	53
BLOOD ROSES KNIT THROUGH MY WEDDING SKIRT	55
I BECOME THE WORLD'S FEROCIOUS LOVER	58
DO NOT DISRUPT YOUR PATTERN	59
BENEATH FOCAL SUN	61
WHITE WHALE	62
NO CIRCUMSTANCE ELIMINATES LIGHT'S SPECTRUM	63
SUN'S OCEAN	65
THE SONGS INSIDE THE MUSIC CABINET	67
THE DESERT	68
THE DESERT	69
THE DESERT	70
THE EVENNESS OF HIM EVERYWHERE	72
DISARRAY THE SENSES	75
LIGHTNING GOES THROUGH LEAVING	77
ANCESTRY	78
MOUNTAINS DETERIORATE ENTIRELY	79
FRAME-FIELD	80
FROM ALL OF SPACE WITH GALAXY CLOUDS	83
THE MAP	84

THE TRANSFER TREE

THANK YOU

unending family of friends, relatives, and poets for giving support, especially Doug Martsch and Ben Youtz.

Adrian Kien and Brandon Shimoda for providing figurative and literal space for the creation of this book.

Sandra and Ben Doller for offering the book's possibility and ensuring its completion/existence.

Monisha Lundquist for your depth content.

Don Mee Choi, Brandon Shimoda, and Cathy Wagner for kindly, generously reading the manuscript and writing for the back of the book.

Melanie Noel, Janet Holmes, and Bonni Ross.

ACKNOWLEDGMENTS WITH GRATITUDE

MUTHAFUCKA printed an excerpt from *The Transfer Tree*. Ghosts and Projectors Reading Series chapbook included "Public Fruit." "The Black Fire," "Nativity," and "By Accident Tracking Him Where He Went" appeared in *Country Music: An Online Journal of Poetry*. "No Need" and "The Desert" have been invited to *Catch Up*.

More titles from 1913 Press:

Conversities, Dan Beachy-Quick & Srikanth Reddy (2012)
Home/Birth: A Poemic, Arielle Greenberg & Rachel Zucker (2011)
Wonderbender, Diane Wald (2011)
Ozalid, Biswamit Dwibedy (2010)
Sightings, Shin Yu Pai (2007)
Seismosis, John Keene & Christopher Stackhouse (2006)
Read, an anthology of intertranslation, Sarah Riggs & Cole Swensen, eds.
1913 a journal of forms, Issues 1-6

Forthcoming:

Bravura Cool, Jane Lewty (2012)
Strong Suits, Brad Flis (2012)
Kala Pani, Monica Mody (2012)
Hg-the liquid, Ward Tietz (2012)
Big House/Disclosure, Mendi & Keith Obadike (2012)
Four Electric Ghosts, Mendi & Keith Obadike (2012)
The Wrong Book, Nathaniel Otting (2013)

1913 titles are distributed solely by Small Press Distribution
www.spdbooks.org
& printed on recycled papers.

THE FIELD'S UNSECRET NET

No shape is preferred or produced by the sparkling field

and here
we are

A rectangular piece of cloth perfectly folded
into four vertical sections without selvage
                cotton interwoven as

                                the image
  threads its image set   a DNA set imagery like DNA
      set imagery combines
    re-combines
                                  the image set:
field tree sun moon night [unknown] plus (a,b)
an inhabited cacophony, the world

To the round horizon go
                In the middle touch the transfer tree

Religion pledges
abstract future freedom
Needed motion requires the opposite [of ideal]
being exactly
what is experienced

PUBLIC FRUIT

The purpose
of this life
is to see directly.

not literally, but current

At the graveyard bones and ashes
are named by stones to
divert the living in liquid electricity

through thousands of orchards

suggest we   pierce the veil

Public love-only prophecy
sounds libertine   I blushed when I watched
the blossom cherish the branch

                but who could love anyone more

                than the tree loves the plum?

PURPLE TREE

At the years-long trial
will anyone prefer me?
Dome of Heaven
Vault of Earth

A juror or a lawyer?

In lavender-orange sunset
will an armed guard take my side enough
that guilt is overlooked and I am
by secure detail seduced

As if romance were a valuable pen pal could I be
cherished though sentenced? At these procedures
where I lose
often and again, a stenographer might witness in
a fractured light
or fragment source
a wish in me
not to testify.   Without plea
innocence glares its chiaroscuro
with every culpability.
Task by task it seems I must be convicted
for botching daily jeopardy

Peach glower of the last sideways sun
Late hearing in an after hours high school classroom
For speaker points a debater
argues any tangent to judges

Instructed to prepare
in my defense the limits
I did not even dress
respectably   Outside the closed-door chambers
enough of us wait in powerless suits

During dinner recess a paralegal approaches. Tattered
manila falls from his arms unfolding coded
pages wash the asbestos floor. Leaving
papers where they scatter
he tells me, "Do not to return to the trial.
You could not bear their charges or survive the world's
convictions. Endure your heart," he asks,
"Even if the meted sentence strikes,
your case should be abandoned." Unrequested counsel
I answer placing my hand on the moon
Together we leave the halls of trials

At the orchid-purple hangman's tree, noose with no neck,
gallows fallen and gone, trampled grass
allowed to straighten, the paralegal researcher
assures me, this field

will never host violence,

never affect any harm

or punishment. Skimming the index of the Book of Day

he finds no precedent   and here gives

extreme permission

to lift the eyes

From the ground of the dawn meadow

I cannot depart   Even bent stalks

call to him   He sits beside me

Normal angels
drink purple wine on distant hills
Blue above green
Crystal sense behind the sternum sees
a stormy libretto begin
Enormously resolved thunderclouds and lightning
procure tree-cracking gusts
angels watch with heroic sympathy

"It will not be yourself that looks out through you

Clean being and behold the valley"

EACH SENSE IS A STAR

The dictionary
a dawn sky. How long shall we recline

on the grass of the field brokenhearted
in general and specific catastrophes? The researcher's patience
outlasts the sun. Never would he
use force (or proof)
where he loiters
in the night tree
in the night field
inside night grasses
senses range unwavering   "Follow me," he says
and I go

THE CROSS WAS BAD MOJO

Deeper and deeper into love's torrential activity:
                              hurricanes of love
                          Currents
    open the locked box of my chest
    Inside its populace

in the moon at night by the tree (gallows unpeopled)
on the field all night with him, how long have we waited?
The researcher says "Marry me"
He props the lid of the dark box
                          Like a fish
                          I leap inside

Leagues and centuries away, the patible or crucifix is devised
so finally one cannot lift her gaze
but kisses wooden racks
for worship's splinters in her lips

Deeper and deeper
I swim   The globe sea expands
until I can no longer be fooled by speeches

One old miracle: bring enough from the depths
to nourish a crowd. My friend asks
the opposite: dive alone into storm waves

and do not jinx the future vow
by promising to surface

If I can marry him to live
without dropping our heads
His posture natively correct
Inside nothing pushes him

On the dark field near the tree time does not move
The earth requires no savior//(the earth and moon are our
                                                      saviors)
Shadows reveal unnatural light
from the nimbling
mind   He never
abandons
(do not get in line) (do not shove)
(the subconscious and unconscious are our saviors)
"Marry me"

"Marry me," he says
Once I was frightened
by the void of our wedding bed
Now I say yes

WHY I AM RELUCTANT TO SET A WEDDING DATE

At a nightclub I party dancing
heartbeat pace   perfectly in sync
with a neighboring enemy
Furious heartbeats speed
elbows at complementary angles
tug dramatically
at a mimed prize between us the dance invented
Openhandedly into his pull
I release
the force of the nothing
we battle over   Clutching a win
he spins away

I dance with my father my brother my mother
Into dice-size bits we chop each other
The pieces turn to dancers faster slower stomping
leaping further
round and round
the black caldera
Lightning flashes   We jeté above it
Lightning goes off in our crotches
In the buried night red with our blood
without our thought   motion and choreography

burn   produced   I turn and turn and turn
into my sister's arms   An enemy loves her
I leap into the liquid mirror of him the silver
stream vanishes red and black
he catches me   Pounding rhythm of the staff
blood and shadow
gold flashes
like in the story when tigers race around a palm tree turn to butter
but with no prejudice no ignorance   no interference not a bit
of a priori information//Before we danced
we did not guess anything//
I am not one or any or all of the dancers
Together the most elegant and awful dances
rendered in despair become scenes of the dancers' lives
Black surrounding mountains
sturdy in the night storm's joy
enclosed
by layers of angels
their white-gold periphery
                            who feel our grief
still register of the dance of the world
the angels'
unutterable quiescence in
the center of the spin   the dancers whirl
Not one could stumble nor one regret
None disconnect
from the dance   layers of dancers, layers of song,

layers of rhythms and steps

Within watching angels the red dance churns the dark valley

THE GREEN INSIDE THE SUN

Field's birthday celebrated
only by sun, bright grass populace
and tree strung with sun internally
throughout my friend
who is the sun. Inside himself
he predicts his action;
sun born with an earth in its center
lives throughout the field. On tree limbs, his legs
dangling,
he sits the sun who born him oh! much light

Extra fields.
I stand on the grass reaching to his feet. Automatically with him
climbing the trunk (central) (an axis-
access   like the old birch)
axis of the field where earth, caelum (sky as ceiling),
underground   we climb like children
at the tree top
one reaches up
to the sky
instantly lifts   Whoosh from the field outside the sun
past the air among stars no body, but the night
between burning
through all of space with
unleashed gape

Above a tiger's jowl
stars pop from nothing
The mouth of night   night
draws negating
gasps as it
whisks away
Automatically the stars no longer a possibility
since they exist we are inside them
our gaping no longer
contained
automatically the blackness by the tiger
bit   The paralegal lifts my chin (my eyes
follow), "You yourself become the automatic
of me."
Won't his speaking ever come out of the night?

White in a white tree
Black in a black tree
Where's the access?   "Remember me
into the drawing motion
through night's jaw. I follow your thought
into the mouth, the crunch, then no sound
of the old world being forgotten. We have leapt
past the sun. Why would you bother to remember?"
The moon.
For you cannot be disrupted.

STARLET

Yearning for the researcher
I obscure him
How does fidelity appear? Stripped to the bones, flesh
incinerated in star furnaces, longing
abrades my body. How can I see him? Without one
object. From every quality
he extricates the longing
scrapes. A container of
electric snaps: vein-nets float outside light
in an accurate translation every appearance
presents the true figure
Apprehend material in a dream
allstuffpressedtogetherasoccurrence   Disappointed
    I lay my forehead on my palm on the
doubleness
dichotomy
False void to be deflected from
Nest at the center of what is gone

CANNOT BE TRANSPORTED OR PRESERVED

Interior gray boulder --
altar in the belly --
fine grained igneous cant top
A big rock to be
broken up. For now, petal by petal I lay out
the flower flag on its plutonic table
in undulating bands, orogons, spirograms.
For hours and days
I pluck bouquets
onto granite at the pine forest's edge --
inside the meadow --
Under the sky: wildflowers', cultivated tulips' and roses' petals
fresh and seashell-curved violet, pastel, yellow, pale pink,
peach, robin's egg onto the stone in layers
and shapes complete in the instant
everything but the flower flag
disappears in navy space

FELT SENSE RECONVENES

Come to us, the angels say, Now we safely celebrate
complete loss. The world will never be okay.

Rounds of seraphim in every form
inhabit most dimensions. Vacuums thick and dazzling
with radiant beings. Is their chorus a translation?
But you have to leave to hear, angels gesture
past the boulevards to jewel atmospheres.

Isn't it impractical, I ask,
to live as one dead? To relinquish the balance sheet?
Turn the stray organism over to humanity?

Scarlet rubies,
sapphires, emeralds, topaz, garnet, carnelian,
unclothed matter-free bodies shape space and color
release to us in the radiate sky
a net no one ties or tests

FIELD HERE

Dark darkness. Bright darkness. Field here.
The cube, stable.
Vertical geometric series through the body:
one X's center: minute sphere
at the throat's cloud. Two textures:
fine-grain and plume
A gold screen with pearl script names
mi cospiri, *my lover is with whom I share my breath.*

Though I am to be cast aside
the green field saturates
polar center set in solid blackness cannot be uprooted
Blackness of the closed at the base lifts to
plenum darkness of the possible.
It's [not] sad [it's sad]; she has to die; she asks,
(metaphorically!? [I hope]) "Who wields the knife?"

Unobserved, break from the stone and become
"a madman or misfit in the world"*. The cloth of story
has been pulled away. No face or event
predicts an imprint. Life has not been shrouded
nor pronounced

Dear, come cutting through the light
Mi cospiri undoes bands and strings across the heart, snaps

with the tip of a blade
cords of centuries

as upon breath

I rely upon him

the tree upon water nutrients sunlight soil air night

*Henry Corbin

AN "EARTH OF LIGHT"
THE LIFE FORCE UNFORCED

Loosely knot around the waist under
no control   I asked the egg or white mouse
in my left palm up my arm
Who can control either?
Imagine how much a snake feels
through the emerald field   how full it glides
to the tree
where the woman stations eager
to climb   The light looses darkness
A shadow cloaks, reveals, delineating
what to cast to the field -- our ground
before Eden, its timeless increation --
every shape
can be accessed
I stay
on the ladder
of the tree   To tame the snake
step to
the ground   It wears no crown
My friend wears the diadem of stars   I wear his voice
From an earth of light he cuts cloth
With the snake unhurt as my belt
he dresses me in a warm coat and long shirts

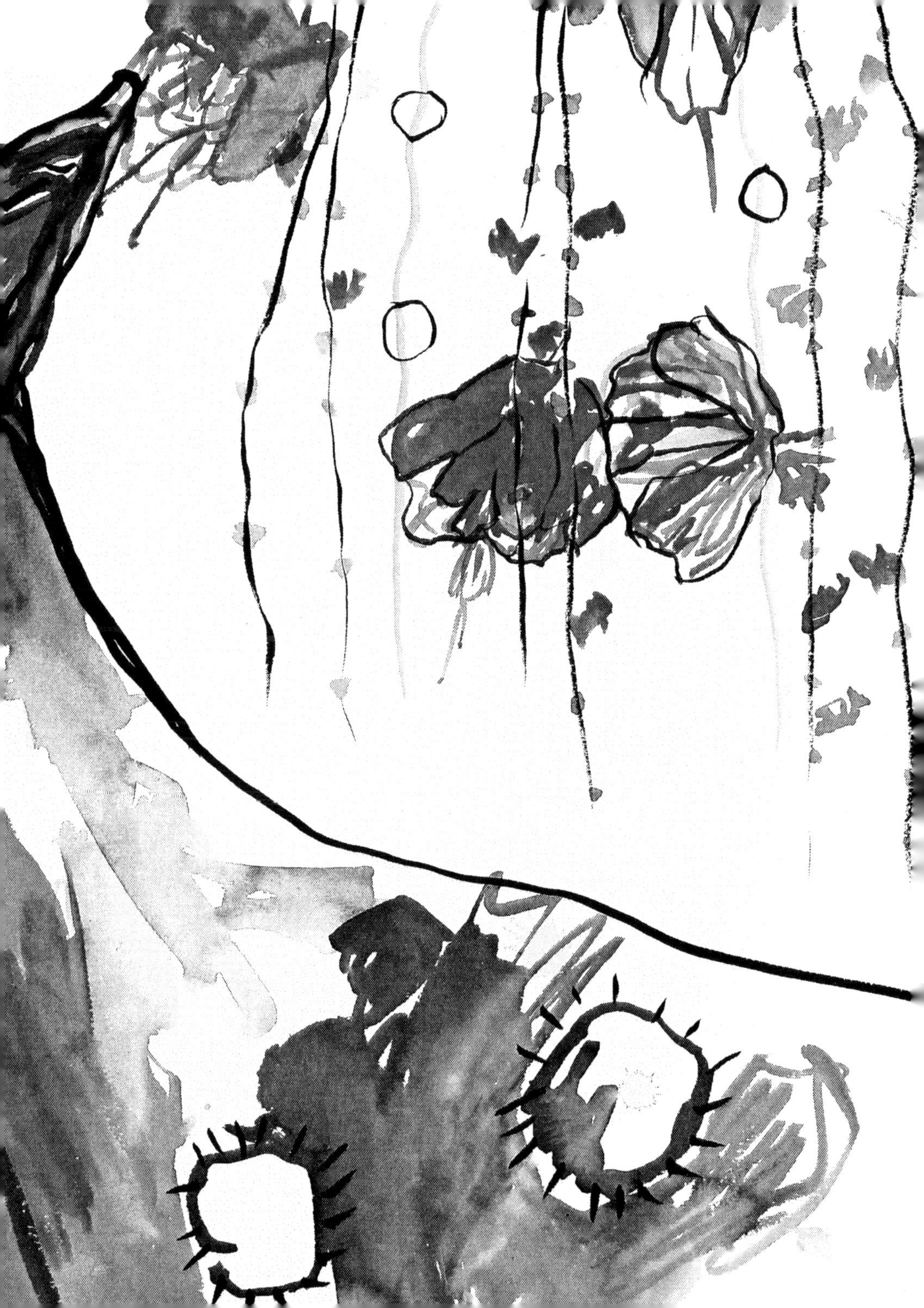

The researcher would never let me be shamed or tamed
even while I feel everything the snake feels
as it takes the egg in its hinged mouth
the unswallowed egg (or mouse)

NO NEED

No need to redeem or consist with
the powers of this world. By its heart-void
the tree is broken through. If the body
wears no semblance   though chopped apart
it cannot be attacked
Hollow trunk upon the grass field
Broken tree where lightning struck
Isosceles triangle above its root
The anomaly roils through
Will the field, tree, and I be taken inside?
The researcher robed me in ivory
Before an interstellar quorum the garments drop
I do not wish to be naked flesh and am given
the navy dress, a spacesuit wove in the
groundless color
A deciduous forest burns
From the ash spring saplings   No occurrence or
appearance, nothing has ever been canceled   Since the slashed
forest grew it registered

With smudges of light a creature brushes ash off itself
uproots plants and twirls them in cones
like the universe Hawking thought of   All the shapes
are (in) motion   The world is not
what to reconcile with. The world salts the ashes

SYMBOLS ARE INTERNAL FACTS

In Blue-Black the concerto's note storm
swathes gray ragged sleeves
trail with rain. Cracked onyx of my lover's
forehead diadem
pours down my arms. A hand over my mouth.
(Even subtle
unkindness stops.) In and from his palm
my friend tosses a coin of light.
Electrons in the cloud
vibrate. The tree is shocked; its void eradicates
burgeoning emblems. Material blackness
resolved by alteration:
a spot for reception
of lightning in my chest. The blast hits
behind the sternum.

No one can make anything
sacred. That would be a hollow filled. The paralegal's
absence cannot be apprehended. I try to
brush away lines of ink
as if they were dust

SONG CONTEST

Planes playing plate-flat fire
plein the
crystal cave where everything
                              is kept
in information matrices

Through space which does not prefer
the tree extends equally.
Rational-material's not an
accurate limit of observation   If there's a door to solid
darkness   do not cross its frame.

WHITE TREE IN NAVY SPACE

The her or room's
dissolving colors we were oriented to firm

A newly fetal body gestates folded
around a star whose pure sphere
registers birth: its disk for
everything to happen can be bit
by spark   a still fire
lain or drawn
every name we knew or did not know
inscribed indestructible

Do we live without the lost? Have we separated?
Impossibility of returning
to anyplace
where they did not exist

Unfilled names wear no more way to occur
nor can they approach the tree whose light threads
an upright body
The vertical line does not combust or devour
The tree sends upwards uncorrupting fire

through shifts of sunrise

COVERED WITH ASHES?

Crude monster chained by wrists with
slack iron links bolted to square
steel plates on the poured
wall. The brute's roars
tear the ranch house off its foundation. I want to see
why the monster's raging, if there's
anything that can be done for him. Starting down
cement stairs his bellowing turns to
baby cries. Onto the basement floor the ogre shrinks
inside its giant manacle and there, as an
ash-covered infant, gripes. Who is this enraged child?
Whose is this? everyone poignantly pointedly denies
connection to the red thing
From the curve of the cuff I lift the baby   My arms
get greasy with monster ashes and my lips where I
                              kiss it, also
my hands where I brush soot from her mouth and eyes
From a broken water main a thick stream
washes us not removing ashes
washes ashes while they stick

Psyches and souls are not demarcated or material are not
rationally real. The monster struggled
structure off. I stand cradling it
with clean ashes inside roofless walls

where the impotent creature had been locked

as the infant's simple, slow,

uninformed caregiver

A pink living dot like an egg or a cell

Chaos a pattern

waiting to happen

RESTLESS

Loyalty occurs
in crowded rooms, the vital betrayals
so physically intimate they have to be kissed.
The paralegal speaks
unsealed language in our tongue to be
in-between-us an image
embossed white upon the sternum's non-gap
But by malperception I turn from him
standing too close to recognize my friend
utterly regarded just where we met by appearing

Delivering sentences upon myself
whom the world mispronounced which coated my heart
like a teflon target
to deflect its own longing   Weather snows and melts
at once;
its drip
tap taps

the home-roof of my cardboard box

How does a living one become transparent enough?
Terrain communes. Because we can it seems we must
go forward with our lamp   Wind traces the world's breaking,
alarming cracks with its high, whispered siren

A microcosm,
just one breaks, finds the sound of an ending
hushed   how one   how everyone exiled from touch
quiets and denies

the wind against the skin

too secret to be betrayed, unwhisperable
existence exactly like
a tree or moon   exactly like a stone or sun
into existence never betrayed

THROUGH

The tree's

initial strand -- straight not taut -- its reed-

hollow bright for seeing

Electrons of every perception

vibrate according attention   All shapes

forth, appear

layers/dimensions of the field

The light conveys

the jot,

dots

beneath condition

Right when

I promise, paralegal researcher, never again to betray you

two owls fly through the yard's winter

walnut tree   Against the rose-purple night sky one

owl dives

THIS IS THE VERSO

Sourceless light with no dominion or compulsion.
Emerald snake through vacant lawn
drops loose into the rectangular hole
for hours
coils the satin reptile

Wracked in cuffs on the basement wall
the monster sighs
Locked in the patible, the horror's just a girl
Curling upon its anguiform
the snake cracks aggregate
bonded with cement   Gray foundation crumbles
Concrete walls collapse,
trapping lucidation,

preventing extension.

(Apperception and hallucination differ how?)

The light and its flames go dumb
The hearing and sight have been pinned

PAIN HAS MINIONS-ARMIES

Trapped, I have to be able to
hallucinate and not believe it
also perceive and accept

After caving in the basement, the emerald snake
demands to be
shaken through
the body's absorbed story, a 3,300 year warning
to suffer. No, do not acquiesce until someone pale
                                        digs you up.
Let the snake
slip through.
Do not tolerate a well when it crumbles

The researcher
undoes my shirt   Life spills out
all over the rubble   "I can never hurt you," he says
and when I am not destroyed by his touch
I do not abandon myself to him.
With no template he yet conveys --
again and again --
I will not be destroyed.
Also, I will be destroyed.
He knows
all the laws

all the sorrow of false law

Breathing dust,
out we crawl

ASHES FALL FROM THE SKY

Padlocked into the charred patible
the eyes cannot be lifted. I do not forget
yet cannot run
to the field. My body
welded to iron. Far from the public square, sorrow falls
onto earth

The world's prisoner
cannot escape. The researcher visits. Hello. Fast
I ask him how best
to hang my head. "Forget everything," he feeds me water then
unlocks the beam's wooden cuffs,
"Forget that it's time to walk
far in the night,
a black hood
over your head
so you do not see
the method. Leaving the trials, you became defenseless;
prior to your appearance the sentence was meted.
I bet you never found
comfort in the world."

Blind, I feel forward beside him.

PEEK OUT OF THE BLACK HOOD INTO ABJECT DARKNESS, FEEL FURTHER (THE SPLIT BRANCH'S FIST-SIZED BOLE)

He talks me through: "Want fear
to be of something? Want reasons
it would not be interesting
to reduce? You chose to
walk the long way
in cinder-shiny dark, not to
designate terror
as missing the target
or assault or armies
or private lack or weight. You walked here
to drop the sternum's leftover."

Where are we?
"In a place where men kill trees and shred living branches.
If I lit this country up,
there would be nothing to torch."
Go ahead, light it up.
"Give me
the charcoal bole."
Show me how to extricate it.
"Just hand it over. Stumble to me in the dark.
Spill the bottomless cup."

Oh. You must be my real and willing lover. I walk an inch.
"Give me yourself." Shaking from billions of us
"Give me all the stuff."
You're not going to light it up?
"No. This will always be dark.
This is stuff. Dear," through the hood he holds
my face in his palms, "You will never understand."

The night does not end trust.
Blindness with him
brighter than day   Neither of us
dark or light   Purgation in the dark
cannot I.D.

NO SUBSTANCE NO DARKNESS

Run to the field, not to
matter or substantial light   Plant or embed
therein the cinder's
vertebral round
Inside the chest live empty
Cast.
material blackness

A black whale swims straight up
through current busts the surface
cetacean cephalized to red and black sky.
Unpronounced apocalypse   Inside yourself,
you never exist
Lights extinguish
eyes and ears
drop away   the mouth   burnt-out tree
a charred circle
upon the field   On the circle a vertical
black triangle   Geometry: measured earth
drops plumb an oriented /center/
through the body's location
stays our void
Profound trust
that we would
reappear:

the pain purged

by unrecording it   understanding purged

by unknowing it   images purged

He removes the hood the ache and stuff wash away

Never sad when I see his face

He does not enter the world

but draws

everything in it to him

The night away from him and the night together

differ like day

One need not approximate

the ground   but traverse

patterns, and patterns of

                                        patterns

THE BLACK FIRE

In blackness on blackness at the grass's green edge
a campfire
fluctuates
teepee of wood
Black fire erupts
crystalline polyhedron night-permeated
appears multiple two tetrahedrons base
to base transparent through one another
red &
black in the fire
no figures
measure
In the fire the alphabet
becomes permanent and cleansed
To adapt to [t]his alphabet
the researcher pushes me into flames

Absent letters
from my body
fall

NATIVITY

Vertical before his body
as the moon the researcher presents
an eight foot tall book
with day-red cover.

Should I crawl into the book? It's spotless. Could I stay
like stone-colored and jelly-colored
jewels affixed to the textless manual?
But he did not press
or inscribe
any imprint   no type of existence

will answer a question unless I ask

The unique edition's spine holds
open love who bears the book's
folio
foliage of the tree in navy space
He has unwritten,
"In this volume
nothing is drawn and I have not failed to be known.
Remember, without one quanta, I transfixed your attention."
Doubtless here I recall
his constant arrival

which could never be converted

into crumbs   though he offers
blank evidence

URSA MAJOR AND URSA MINOR

Syllable weft of two grass blades
Multiple
lulling syllables
of the field
where we recline   Drops chime and Bell of stars
Flowercups
Beneath the tree we embrace   Shhhh
his finger indexes my mouth   his mouth counts my mouth,
one.

I forget earth   It remembers itself   The field
holds us   Brown ground whose hues are tones
Inside the tree, earth,
and space strung with every
strand of song

    //oh! of the whole universe//

THE BINDING OF THE BUD

None require birth   Songs pre-exist
Underground Spring develops
unnecessary flowers, bark for the birch, skin for
me, squirrel fur.
Tulip, egg, daffodil, and leaf surfaces
arrive in two months
unconstrained by birth to live
prior existence reviving the field

To listen to songs I attempt not to
dream or battle   lay down my laudanum and my
giant axe   The field drinks and chops

HOW NOT TO BE BORN

The researcher jumps into my nerves and bones   If I stay
with him I need not be born

RAPIDITY

(phenomenons draw toward one another)

Subject no longer automatic   Tiger on the field
paw near its face, pearl in its teeth: the sleek thing
leaps
into night the snake evacuates its casing
The researcher asks, "What did you want?"
People pull unneeded
bluff from their limbs/torsos and set it down like
jewels in light   The field suffuses
auroral sky   A whole town climbs into the tree
except a few of us remain
as bowls on the field   guessing
what we might receive
My friend ahems,
"Enjoy some humility doll-shaped casket. Love
just now is not dynamic."   Information over and
through an ocean wash a little

                              room's roof
and rain skin. "Again and again I have asked you,"
he holds my hands
tight, I was trying to push him, "Not to defend yourself."
With expert judo he continues to hold
while I shove and fight,

to keep close and let neither of us
be bruised

"But you don't know," I pant, wearing out,
"It hurts so much." He grabs the black cup and
shatters it onto the field as
a thousand onyx diamonds
it radiates.   A parable: upright
unburdened posture of his unbound body --
an obscene beautiful beacon --
I crave him.

The broken vessel
has dissolved   How can he
be received?   Into
all of space an
uncentered universe
the predator jumps through night's door

to be encompassed by him

BY ACCIDENT TRACKING HIM WHERE HE WENT

Following the paralegal's vanish I stop
transplace
without manifest quiet and wide   Full of
/images flash to life/ a continuum does not dream or
decide. The extra that awaits
before signs occur is us
No auteur to hew appearance, just
a shared quality at
/begin to exist/   Search   How might I cross here?
Images
/Begin/ back behind the signs not in a glyphed cave---
I need to paint a cave---signlessness
not at all space or color   Points of attention
vanish into attention
canceling perception   The book proffered with
no object does not persist   Backwards
through my forehead he speaks past a /place/ where
timeless signs have yet to shift
to his priority
Much deeper in ether the place
does not contrast
Every connection he gaps
as meaning

but the place of /yet to/ does not.
On the other side someone might request a sign
but from him none exist
the tree
the field
the snake
sphere   him, me

native actions   deep law
gravity impersonal

in constancy's similitude
or fact of love from
infra-red A to ultra-violet Z,
a spectral alphabet
impossible on his page of the absences
whose signs are never transitive

RARE MINERAL AND THE SOCIAL STRUCTURE

Black purple blue brown sorry no credit cards only cash
for fuel to the destination, sorry.
I want
space
unlimited. Here, I thrust to the paralegal a cluster
crystal apricot and creamy with spectral gleaming
rose to violet jonquil bluebonnet colors
seaming
iridescent green strands near the inorganic surface
"Give it back to me if you don't want it anymore," I say.
"Hey," he answers, "I still bite."
We have agreed to attend a religious feast.
From the truckstop bathroom, I notice my red purse
has been stolen, its cash clothes jewels
left in a neat stack on the porcelain sink
but I do need
just in case
the container
though I gave away the mineral.

Huge meal at a round table. The researcher sits distant;
a religious leader prays. I space out The Feast
of World Annunciation Day. In the dimmed room

guests chat and chew. From seatmates I wish
not to be diminished
nor augmented my place at the table
canceled by talking over others the taking over of others
Problematic shy person's negative dominion
I lean into: where to establish myself? Suddenly
I'm colonized a missionary starts conversing. Four men
individually possess manifest destiny over
every person in the room.

By social convention the paralegal and I were seated far
from one another. I do not regret
I gave him irreplaceable minerals
when the next person asks, "What do you do?"

I give away my rarest possession.

I wait for my friend.

Across the party he is covered by a shadow

I ask my dinner companion the same question.
Somehow she might make
our aloneness speak

BLOOD ROSES KNIT THROUGH MY WEDDING SKIRT

The Rose in the Crucible: from crisp cloth
of my wedding skirts four roses' circumferences
have been die-cut & blood-red roses therein
attached.

A whole-town festival
marrying three or four brides requiring
thousands of square pieces of bridal cake
in the town square near the fountain as well as real champagne.
Children dress in jackets or embroidered velvet.
Neither the feast
nor the wedding
could I attend. While I flee roses dry
to reddish purplish brown. In windowless quiet
of a row house I hide with its metal door soft shut.

For less than one hour I extend this lonesome wait,
then sneak out for cake. Vows have not yet
been exchanged though the white confection is cut and
blood-red roses in my skirts dried dark

Rudely and accidentally I almost
in my gown observe

another's nuptials, but the bride
behind her veil
cannot notice me at her ceremony   I remember
my dowry
was already
transferred with the dress's stains figured in:
skirts and bodice, slips
and shift glaringly
white with merry
blood colored roses   their telling blood from long ago
The rose in the crucible   Vows not yet spoken
Guests about to sweep in
Empty square with thousands of square pieces, white bridal
cake prepared and brought before the fountain.
Vows to speak, Vows spoken   Dowry offered, Dowry gone
Dark-colored roses crocheted in the gown

But if she does not speak, the townspeople murmur of me,
Surely there will be no vow to keep
"My mouth is filled with cake," I mumble to the researcher.
When he asks for my word I will not look
in his eyes he and I
stare down at the roses   "Okay,"
he whispers, holding my hand before
the jovial crowd still gathering. Unembarrassed
that I would not pledge, he addresses guests,

"She will not speak of me
so I for her and for myself
these roses receive." Our marriage
would leave me
completely white

Now the paralegal
considers himself
spoken for

I BECOME THE WORLD'S FEROCIOUS LOVER

The black and purple spherical bomb cracks in half to
reveal no inner workings
No longer do I wish to be
subject to myself or kept in line.
From the town square I run
A fashionista packed my suitcase room to room
and town to town for a birth death birth death etc.
rage through tourist traps [the universe]
Loving every meal I tear fearfibers shred
embrace wildly as the tiger the fawn
rips apart the sweatshirt to its central
you, not the tension of
keeping myself in line. Slaughtering pigs of non-love
I toss carcasses to starving carnivores
of the desiccated forests   I violate my person style
ideas and bodies   I violate
my separation   I violate
the vow I would not make by keeping it
All the worlds turn and break
at my throat
the way my lover loves   unchecked and complete

DO NOT DISRUPT YOUR PATTERN

Kneeling beside the lake I toss petals
onto its surface the flower flag configures

Is the current?
Shapes accrue the day sky's
accurate reflection
Plucked flowers and living flowers line up
the rose's spiral
elevates the pond
I curl up in long
sticky-sharp grasses gray-green, lightly clacking.
Smell of willows
The undisrupted pattern forms,
fragments, resolves   Sun folds up its cloth and
the flower-flag drifts   Ashore
silt washed by lapping beneath minute green organisms
bound in tattered curtains afloat wavelets
Crystalline, even the organic pattern, action of earth
already: carp, wood duck, frogs, wild small irises
in fevered eyes; sight altered
I greet the researcher   Leaning
forward he kisses
my fortress eyelids   His voice
whirls through the skull withdrawing
distortion

and the eye or ear
does not begin
to guess itself and the tongue and touch
are not predicted

BENEATH FOCAL SUN

The researcher and I throw our laundry
into red lava; his pastiche
requires a new job for him
with work clothes and trans-Atlantic commute
At the hub central to spoke-hallways and streets we meet

With hot lava
to wash clothes in
to instant cinders, he shows
how he pools himself
though I stand between us
preventing union

He digs his hand into my thigh
"Go down to the reeds
in the water." His touch
in my bone streams   "Purify yourself
                    and receive the sign"

WHITE WHALE

From leagues below
the behemoth surfaces. Rain stops light on the window.

No Captain with
a clean little autumn
Someone furnished her a white tree
to lean against, climb upon, and be sheltered by, also
navy cloth of all space for a dress

Everything she heard was given to her and she remembers this.

Navy space, field,
circumference grasses, length tree
whose vertex
increases
branches of everything we need   Arms open
give or receive

The root through the soil
does never diminish
so deep into earth
runs stabilizing darkness

NO CIRCUMSTANCE ELIMINATES LIGHT'S SPECTRUM

If anyone asks, what are the shapes of light?
Answer with earth

The "Biggest Moon of the Year" tripped
western horizon with its fat cake. Now day's
burrowed clouds regulate fertile acres

Pull yards of ribbon and thin
silver from behind the sternum, petal threads of
mercurial length   Cloth once bound me
then my friend unanchored shining strings
Is winding loosely
wrapping into cords and braids mine?
The paralegal, not touching, draws me to him
Not one floss knots   The earth illuminates itself and
I am not wove in or roped I am not
cut   unplied pliable lines

                let

alone

into space

ungather   a white tree's

                              vertical yield.

                You and me
                              like craters
                    on

                         a   huge

                    moon

SUN'S OCEAN

A shoe-box sized cabinet floats near my chin and
konks my cheek bone. The tiny door
knocks my jaw
a few times so I go in
through the gold vortex, a flexible loose tube
leading
in and out of the cupboard   In the gold ocean
everything drifts
connected
From deeps the behemoth swims straight up swallows
treading   pulls me
down solid.
Sand floor   By the motion of the current
through the cabinet I could leave
but stay
like waves below
stable on the ocean floor

White and colorful vertical concourses:
one in
the exact middle

Far beneath sight and sound the filament's curious
without
jostling

touches pleasant pelvic seat
where the whale dragged devouring
straight up straight down
vertical paths and spiral tubes
travel anywhere   even to the world
in the darkness of the gut
with the whale's breath culled and held

On the ocean floor
the researcher's palm unfurls   He and I
the opposite of puppets with our volition
love   all the way under the gold-topped ocean
he connects everything
in unknotted lines

THE SONGS INSIDE THE MUSIC CABINET

are not mine. No dancer

can leap from the dance. To beckoning figures

I turn and turn and turn. Across offered arms release

my spine the song

like a cloud carries us to existence faraway cymbal crashes chant

A dancer spins me   Another lifts me   I run

the ribbons flash   Not one grabs another wrong

None are reined or bound   The Dance of Dawn   pastel

fluorescence   Sweat on the vivid lip

of every participant   rest

in the cadence

of the burst

before the sun clips

which will never happen

as we pause

open-armed the only motion checked breath

to pant and await

THE DESERT

"Go alone."
Translucent membrane of the blank dissolves
me to view
No lightsource. Nothing dark
or nothing bright   Boiled, dried vegetation
from crusted dirt, pocked lava: air and basalt
walk any distance and meet
quartz sand   Resources abate   Lizards with
cigarette-sized tails
swallowed by snakes
having the hunger
removed
Beige plain on the periphery of
town. The world's colors press and stretch within
intact membranes   Placeless I wander and
do not search
for an entrance   Though exhausted, walk.

The researcher gave me
a note to open
as soon as I forget the note

THE DESERT

To enter the unwanting desert, a land's bare thin
diaphanous sun
disperse through a hole in light
one cannot seek him   He comes from
noplace which seeks him   Earlier, between us,
there had been an argument: He asked,
"What did you do with the medallions I gave you?"
I shook my head, "They're gone."

I wish I remembered if I did
place some in people's hands. He stops protecting me
from shame.

"The coins?"
Gone.

"The field?"

"The tree?"

"Your dress?"

gone gone gone

"Go alone"

THE DESERT

I want to walk
as deep as he into the wind where
wind begins and blows no more

A desert before the wind soothes the plain's dry surface
Earth crumbles
Alphabet letters crack apart
poppy chips of glass ash clink
chemical volcanoes. Then sounds abjure
who were not states   He stays.
Knit integral
as the roses in my dress
in body chemistry as the catalyst
the way a dream is full and precise with no element
missing
he remains
This is the hardest of the hard losses;
gold coins he molded wind takes away
In no
infinity or surface
he lives   Cobalt blue ruby red
fuchsia ochre crouch hidden in light
Light encounters what does not contain it
colors appear

The desert's sourceless   Unwavering saturate --
similitude's pallor --
Contain every color
and none appear
where the spectrum finds no absence to reveal

THE EVENNESS OF HIM EVERYWHERE

White pole
people careen around
to long for
verticality's
ver
ti
cal
dislodging   To be disheveled with the researcher
in the center of his body where no wound can touch
nor a cancer or infection

A white book with spectral letters   Fewer than one% of
colors are named   A polar glaze of
sparkling matte varnish

In the mountain town surrounding the black monolith
dirt and sandstone cliffs' erosion threatens condos
Striations in the monolith's gleaming
rise stories above ski runs
black diamond level tiger striped with pine trees
At the monolith's base begin to measure
stories above the ridges,
the center of the physical world anchored
in stone-stuff, a pilgrimage place

to circumambulate. The monolith
never lets us in. Round and round the solid
we do dream, shuffle, and throw
our minds all over material   Not to deny
humility in the eyes-down quality
of the worshippers of the world   Each pays
ferry-fare or sin tax and trudges deadly.
Black cornerstone of the world's foundation,
imposed magnet draws us as
opposite charges   Inescapable mimesis
walking around and around the base

One slogs one's pilgrimage and never enters perhaps
allowed to ascend
to the stone-top   but our upright tree embraces
ascent   enclosure
        Consent becomes
constant   invisible
stalk-thin   unloseable

Names inscribed in the black stone
in the world's encrypted script make secrets

The sturdy base. Relentless. Could not punch through it
ignore it throw it away could not want the cornerstone
removed its monolith anchors all construction

In the physical center one cannot be unpossessed.
In stories told at the stone
which cannot hear or know
love among people obscures the obvious
such as wheel-like motion around and around the stone

DISARRAY THE SENSES

Unless you are a blue heron why are you trying to sneak up
behind the frog and kill her among
cattails of a manmade lake?

The black monolith rises from the lake's center
its solid tomb impenetrable
as structure itself: physical sign, lack of entity
Outer center: matter, utter non-comment
Focus forms the body/lake
occurs at once attention arranges
placed instantly orients anyplace/no time without
our effort to ignore
While not denying the rock cannot reflect
I want to learn
amphibious element switch
the rock not permanent but apparent
mystery of material as the least fluid sign---
The dream has structure---
The monolith's immense indifference
[Like the Financial Giant Blackrock or Mercenary
Blackwater]: the monolith's inverse numinosity does not
tower in my trajectory but at the polar center
of the physical world
I'm seeing
the opposite

of him

The black monolith tangible result hard evidence outward
central and huge, overwhelming
facts I do not consider   A bad mistake
to enter statistical material and empirical data
for the mind to be frozen in   Even on the rock itself,
some devanagari reads, Do not go in here

Do not even stand near the rock

Lightning goes through leaving
inside the tree electricity
too fast to charred darkness
empty   Grass, unstruck, straightens
green all around

The muscle's relevance   Agility's relevance
no longer conduct
electrons, their charge against what disappears
Ability to comment sets one
apart   Hold away the night
and become

When the light has torn through to no more made
or affected light
the forests' really loose constructions

an angel would have to wrestle me through all eternity
to get me to give up

ANCESTRY

Regular Genealogy: DNA   but within the tree, no inherited chains

I jump into its hollow and tumble underground

Beneath the roots and field
my real family embrace me

MOUNTAINS DETERIORATE ENTIRELY

Until the dance begins no person lives in all of space
The valley disappears so we dance,
suspended in one another

A caldera splinters; no injury could exile anyone
Inside the dance no one has ever been harmed
The one who chose me
lifts me through placeless sun
Our wedding feast is yet to come, the night
in our lives we dance first, alone, as one

FRAME-FIELD

Frame-field disperse.
Loose gold knit in navy space
Life
being given
another kind of life, immiscible

//green fields in near air
a new chemical or
molecular Eden//   the moon's closeness

A red squirrel with long, ragged fur totes
potatoes from thrown out soup
along the privacy fence   its tail stripped

Image as spoke-through or say-through
cast net to catch nothing   it does stable
                                   not drift
                                                         or disrupt
drafts and winds of space   high whirring arcs
                                   of traffic engines

The morning's walnut tree, anglewires, and muddy grass so bright
the yard might not
be real, but vivid
bringing-in almost

beneath sight (to see feel hear touch [again] taste)
We do not speak of it for we do not know a separate one
to speak to: knit grid, residential buildings,
a most secure possible golden cube

If every thought has a shape or identity or is
                                            identifiable
he identifies himself
    integrates himself
                unthought

The grid/net's non-disruption

Our other names are called
Reply in the lines
The grid is care
Do I feel? Yes. I will never disrupt.
He stays even with the wars
                and radiation

A sun in reverse draws undiminished light to light's source
even if the stuff and skeleton are shaken off
    The unmaintained lawn wore off

Tactile traction

The sun behind the sun when it longs for
its initial state and turns

    Allium-like foliage of the Star of Jerusalem

Shaking inside the sun's gulf
the sun erupts

FROM ALL OF SPACE WITH GALAXY CLOUDS

The one who chose me I choose
Discarded by the world he and I
were not separately imagined

Fast through the tree the researcher
drops me drawing the ground's
transformation; literal
he shows
the way through earth

During our wedding
in one gesture my veil
he shall draw aside
Though he does not observe
my shining dress
until
revealed by him

THE MAP

Without time a task occurs
not placed in opposition to the world

In navy space
at a table without implement
I sit alone
regarding a cobalt and
canary nebula's nascence

Arriving stars part like a curtain

Surprising me with a paper gift
onto the table the researcher
unrolls my new map   Beside my right shoulder he stands
Together we weight the edges
to hold open
terrain.   Inked swamps
Overcome turquoise coasts are currently being altered Island
coves of the oceans' shapes
Jungle flora and fauna   The deserts sift
slim populations   I look to him, "Where?"   He stands
as the moon

Near a once-white pole
the print of his index finger

lands on the key, pointing from
beyond designation -- himself
non-local -- crossed center of eight drawn directions
and innumerable routes to be attempted

Equidistant perpendicular lines
cross a compass-drawn circle
at the elbows, 90 degree angles;
pop it up one further dimension into a sphere.

pewter-colored weight spins
Gravity is a piece of cloth

Waiting for time to begin
to touch one another gathering
inside the translation of how to site the map:
outwardly align with the north star
Internally carry the map to the tree   A vertical
polar or /first/ orientation
must occur   One does not
establish in principalities or territory
but in the key's
infinite navigation into the center of every direction
"Go here," he says, "Into the key."